FUJIFILM
X-T4
POCKET GUIDE

TABLE OF CONTENTS

01 PRE-SHOOT CHECKLIST

Check these settings before you head out with your camera!

SETTING	MY PREFERRED SETTING
☑ Shooting Mode	....
☑ Sensitivity (ISO) Setting	....
☑ White Balance	....
☑ Focus Mode	....
☑ Focus Area	....
☑ Drive Setting	....
☑ Metering Mode	....
☑ Bracketing: On/Off	....
☑ File Format: JPEG, RAW, or RAW+JPEG	....
☑ Image Stabilization	....
☑ Flash Mode	....
☑ Film Simulation	....
☑ Exposure Compensation	....
☑ Battery Fully Charged and In Camera	....
☑ Memory Card(s) Formatted and In Camera	....

02 BUTTONS, DIALS, AND SCREENS

CAMERA BODY TOP

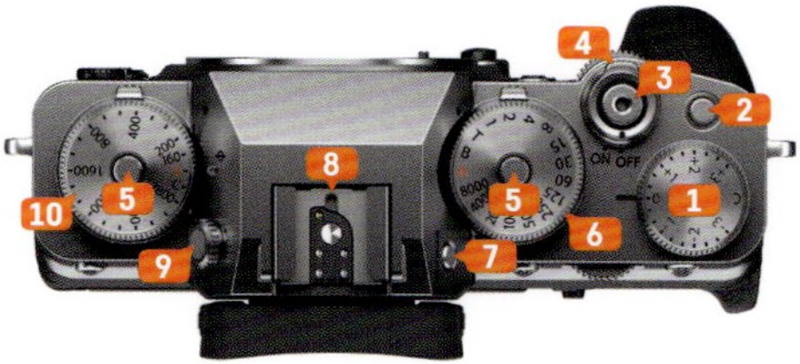

1. **Exposure Compensation Dial:** Adjust exposure compensation amount.
2. **Fn1 Button:** Default is set to Face/Eye Detection.
3. **Shutter Button:** Press to take photo.
4. **On/Off Switch:** Turn the camera on and off.
5. **Dial Lock Release:** Unlock the Shutter Speed dial and the Sensitivity dial.
6. **Shutter Speed Dial:** Set the shutter speed.
7. **View Mode Button:** Cycles through the display modes.
8. **Hot Shoe:** Mounting spot for external flash units.
9. **Diopter Adjustment Control:** Adjust the viewfinder display.
10. **Sensitivity/ISO Dial:** Set the ISO.

CAMERA BODY FRONT

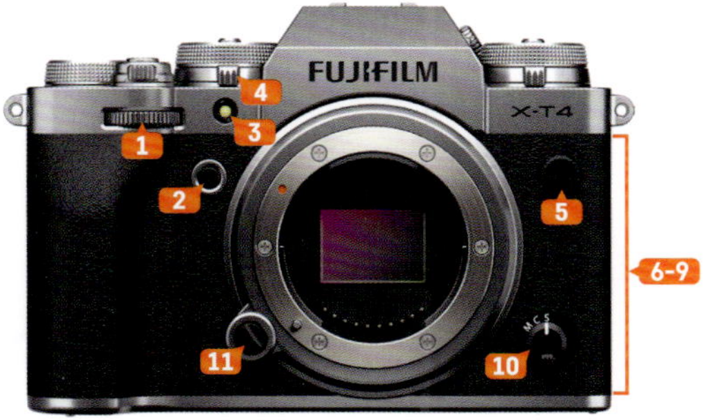

1. **Front Command Dial:** See "Front Command Dial" on page 6.
2. **Fn2 Button:** Default is to control the Drive settings.
3. **AF-assist Lamp/Self-timer Lamp/Tally Light:** Used to help AF in low lighting / show when self-timer is active / can be set to show when movies are being recorded.
4. **Still/Movie Mode Dial:** Used to switch between still and movie modes.
5. **Sync Terminal:** Connect a sync cable.
6. **Microphone Jack:** Used for external microphone.
7. **Remote Release Connector:** Attach a remote cable to the camera.
8. **HDMI Micro Connector:** Plug in HDMI cable (type D).
9. **USB Connector:** Plug in USB Type C cable to connect external devices.
10. **Focus Mode Selector:** Select the Focus mode.
11. **Lens Release Button:** Press to allow the lens to be removed.

CAMERA BODY BACK

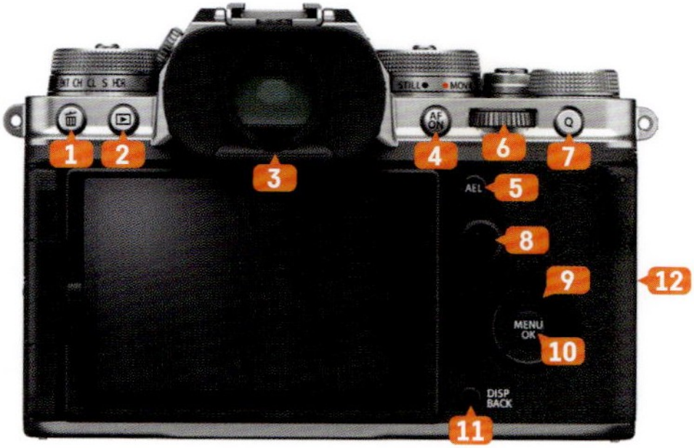

1. **Delete Button:** Press to delete the current image.
2. **Playback Button:** Press to view images on the monitor.
3. **Eye Sensor:** Turns the EVF (electronic viewfinder) on and off based on whether the sensor is covered.
4. **AF ON Button:** Activates the autofocus.
5. **AEL Button:** Default is to lock exposure without locking focus.
6. **Rear Command Dial:** See "Rear Command Dial" section on page 7.
7. **Q (Quick Menu) Button:** Press to open the Quick menu.
8. **Focus Stick:** Use to select the focus area and navigate the menus.
9. **Selector/Fn3–6 Buttons:** Use the Selector buttons to navigate menus. The Up, Right, Down, and Left buttons also serve as the Fn3, Fn4, Fn5, and Fn6 buttons.
10. **MENU/OK Button:** Press to open menu, and use to select current highlighted menu choice. Note: Press and hold to lock or unlock camera buttons.
11. **DISP/BACK Button:** Press to cycle through Display modes, and use to exit menu system.
12. **Memory Card Slots:** The X-T4 has available slots for two SD cards.

CAMERA BODY BOTTOM

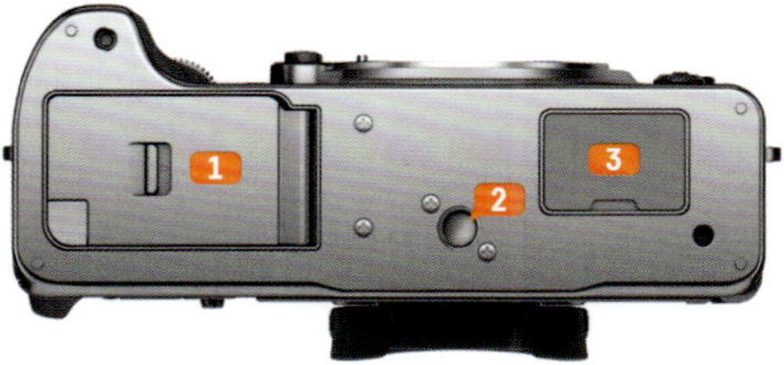

1. **Battery Chamber:** Insert battery.
2. **Tripod Mount:** Standard tripod/monopod mounting hole.
3. **Vertical Battery Grip Connector:** Use to attach an optional vertical grip.

FUNCTION BUTTONS

The X-T4's six Function (Fn) buttons are set to the following default controls.

- **Fn1: Face Detection On/Off:** Turns face detection on or off.
- **Fn2: Drive Settings:** Access the settings used by each of the Drive modes.
- **Fn3: Photometry (Metering Mode):** Sets the metering mode for the camera.
- **Fn4: Film Simulation:** Choose a Film Simulation to apply to the image.
- **Fn5: White Balance:** Access the White Balance menu.
- **Fn6: Performance:** Access the Performance menu to switch between Boost (faster AF speed and viewfinder display), Normal (Normal AF Speed and viewfinder display), and Economy, which limits AF and viewfinder performance but uses less battery power.

COMMAND DIALS

There are two Command dials, which can be rotated or pressed.

Front Command Dial

- Rotate to select menu tabs or pages.
- Rotate to adjust aperture when lens doesn't have an aperture ring, or the lens has an aperture ring and the aperture is set to A (auto) and Command is selected for Button/Dial setting (A).
- Rotate to adjust exposure compensation when the Exposure Compensation dial is set to C.
- Adjust the sensitivity to light (ISO) when the Sensitivity dial is set to C or On is selected for Movie Optimized Control.
- Scroll through images in Playback mode.
- Press to switch between aperture, ISO, and exposure compensation when the sensitivity dial is set to A and the Exposure Compensation dial is set to C.
- You can set the Front Command dial to a custom function in Setup Menus > Button/Dial Setting > Command Dial Setting.

Rear Command Dial

- Rotate to highlight menu items.
- Rotate to choose the aperture and shutter speed combination (Program Shift).
- Rotate to adjust shutter speed (select in Setup Menus > Button/Dial Setting > Command Dial Setting).
- Rotate to adjust settings in the Quick menu.
- Rotate to choose the size of the focus frame.
- Rotate to zoom in or out during either full-frame playback or multi-frame playback.
- Press to perform the function assigned to the Dial function button.
- Press to zoom in on the active focus point (when Focus Check is assigned to a Function button).
- Press and hold to choose the manual focus display (when Focus Check is assigned to a Function button).
- Press to zoom in on an active focus point during playback.

ELECTRONIC VIEWFINDER DISPLAY

Note: **Not all of these items will be displayed at the same time.**

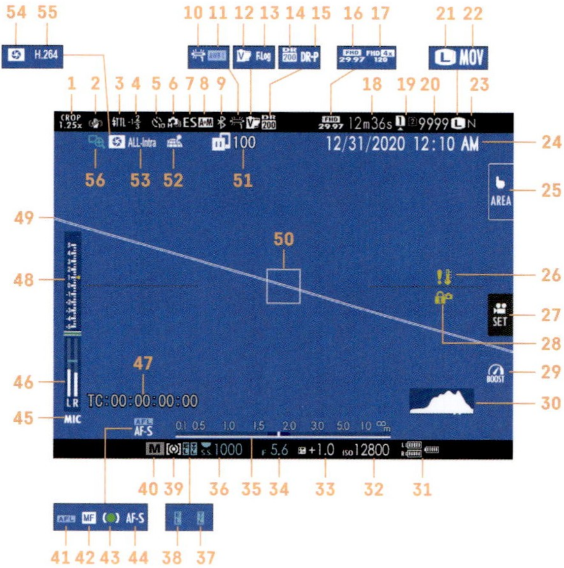

1. Sports Finder Mode: A 1.25x crop mode that is set by selecting Shooting Menus > I.Q. (Image Quality) Setting > Image Size.

2. **IS (Image Stabilization) Mode:** Image Stabilization can be set to Continuous, Shooting Only (only active in Focus mode C or when the shutter is released), or Off.

3. **Flash (TTL) Mode:** Shows the TTL for the EF-X8 hot shoe-mounted flash.

4. **Flash Compensation:** Shows the current amount of flash compensation.

5. **Self-Timer Indicator:** Shows the number of seconds remaining until the camera fires.

6. **Continuous Mode:** Shows which Continuous mode is selected: CH (Continuous High) or CL (Continuous Low).

7. **Shutter Type:** Shows which shutter type is selected.

8. **AF+MF Indicator:** Shows if AF+MF is on or off.

9. **Bluetooth On/Off:** Shows if Bluetooth is on or off.

10. **White Balance:** Shows current White Balance setting.

11. **AWB Lock:** Shows if AWB (Auto White Balance) is locked.

12. **Film Simulation:** Shows the currently selected Film Simulation.

13. **F-Log/HLG Recording:** Shows if F-Log or HLG (Hybrid Log-Gamma) is being used.

14. **Dynamic Range:** Shows Dynamic Range setting.

15. **D-Range Priority:** Shows D-Range setting.

16. **Movie Mode:** Shows the current movie mode (frame rate, bit rate, frame size, and aspect ratio).

17. **Full HD High-Speed Recording:** Shows the current settings used. This allows for slow motion playback.

18. **Time Remaining:** Shows amount of time remaining for movie capture.

19. **Card Slot Options:** When using two memory cards, you can set the cards to work in the following ways:

    Sequential: The second card is used after the first card is filled.

    Backup: Each frame is saved to both cards.

    RAW/JPEG: RAW files are saved to first memory card slot and JPEGs to the second memory card.

20. **Number of Available Frames:** Shows the number of frames that can still be shot using the current settings.
21. **Image Size:** Shows current image size.
22. **File format:** Shows the current file format.
23. **Image Quality:** Shows current image quality.
24. **Date and Time:** Shows current date and time.
25. **Touch Screen Mode:** Shows which touch screen is set (see "Touch Screen Controls" in Section 04).
26. **Temperature Warning:** Shows yellow or red as camera gets too hot. Turn camera off and wait for it to cool down.
27. **Movie Optimized Control:** Shows that controls dials and touch controls are set for movie shooting.
28. **Control Lock:** Shows when controls are locked.
29. **Boost Mode:** Improves viewfinder and AF speed. Shows if this is turned on.
30. **Histogram:** Shows the histogram for the current view.
31. **Battery Level:** Shows power level of battery.
32. **Sensitivity (ISO):** Shows current ISO.
33. **Exposure Compensation:** Shows the current Exposure Compensation.
34. **Aperture:** Shows current aperture.
35. **Distance Indicator:** Shows the distance to the subject.
36. **Shutter Speed:** Shows current shutter speed.
37. **TTL Lock:** Shows when Flash TTL output is locked. Used to keep output consistent over a series of images (Lock with Last Flash, or Lock with Metering Flash).
38. **AE Lock:** Shows when exposure is locked.
39. **Metering:** Shows current Metering mode.
40. **Shooting Mode:** Shows current Shooting mode.
41. **Focus Mode:** Shows current Focus mode.

42. **Focus Indicator:** Shows the focus status.

( ): Camera is focusing.

• (green): Subject is in focus and locked, in S Focus mode.

(•) (green): Subject is in focus in C Focus mode, focus will adjust as subject distance changes.

(•) (blinking white): Camera is unable to find focus.

43. **Manual Focus Indicator:** Shows when you're using Manual focus.
44. **AF Lock:** Shows when autofocus is locked.
45. **Mic Jack Setting:** Shows if a microphone or line in is selected for the mic jack.
46. **Recording Level:** Shows the current audio recording level.
47. **Time Code:** Shows the current time code.
48. **Exposure Indicator:** In M mode it shows how different the current settings are from what the camera believes the proper exposure should be according to the current Metering mode.
49. **Virtual Horizon:** Shows the virtual horizon, allows you to create level images.
50. **Focus Frame:** Shows the area the camera will use to focus.
51. **Image Transfer Status:** Shows the current image transfer status.
52. **Location Data Download Status:** Shows the current data download status.
53. **Movie Compression:** Shows which compression is being used.

ALL-Intra: Each frame is compressed, creating larger files, but good for footage that will be post-processed.

Long GOP: Creates good image quality with high compression, making for smaller file sizes.

54. **Depth-of-Field Preview:** Shows when the Preview Depth of Field is active.
55. **H.265(HEVC)/H.264:** Shows which codec is being used.
56. **Focus Check:** When on, the display will zoom in when the focus ring is rotated in Single AF (AF-S) or Manual focus mode.

LCD MONITOR DISPLAY

Note: **Not all of these items will be displayed at the same time.**

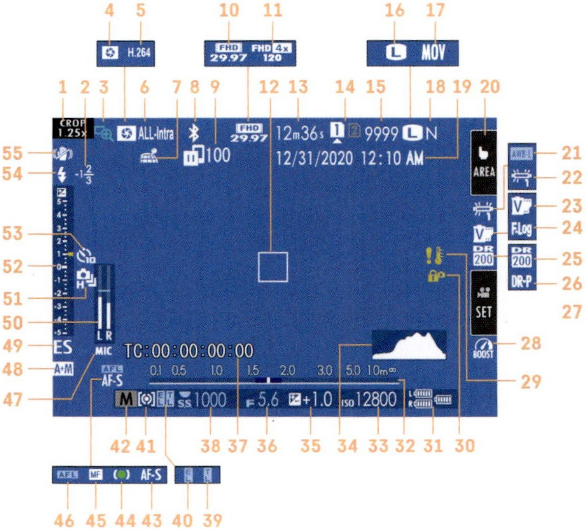

1. Sports Finder Mode: A 1.25x crop mode that is set by selecting Shooting Menus > I.Q. (Image Quality) Setting > Image Size.

2. Flash Compensation: Shows the current amount of flash compensation.

3. **Focus Check:** When on, the display will zoom in when the focus ring is rotated in Single AF (AF-S) or Manual focus mode.

4. **Depth-of-Field Preview:** Shows when the Preview Depth of Field is active.

5. **H.265(HEVC)/H.264:** Shows which codec is being used.

6. **Movie Compression:** Shows which compression is being used.

   ALL-Intra: Each frame is compressed, creating larger files, but good for footage that will be post-processed.

   Long GOP: Creates good image quality with high compression, making for smaller file sizes.

7. **Location Data Download Status:** Shows the current data download status.

8. **Bluetooth On/Off:** Shows if Bluetooth is on or off.

9. **Image Transfer Status:** Shows the current image transfer status.

10. **Movie Mode:** Shows the current movie mode (frame rate, bit rate, frame size, and aspect ratio).

11. **Full HD High-Speed Recording:** Shows the current settings used. This allows for slow motion playback.

12. **Focus Frame:** Shows the area the camera will use to focus.

13. **Time Remaining:** Shows amount of time remaining for movie capture.

14. **Card Slot Options:** When using two memory cards, you can set the cards to work in the following ways:

    Sequential: The second card is used after the first card is filled.

    Backup: Each frame is saved to both cards.

    RAW/JPEG: RAW files are saved to first memory card slot and JPEGs to the second memory card.

15. **Number of Available Frames:** Shows the number of frames that can still be shot using the current settings.

16. **Image Size:** Shows current image size.

17. **File Format:** Shows the current file format.

18. **Image Quality:** Shows current image quality.

19. **Date and Time:** Shows current date and time.

20. **Touch Screen Mode:** Shows which touch screen is set (see "Touch Screen Controls" in Section 04).
21. **AWB Lock:** Shows if AWB (Auto White Balance) is locked.
22. **White Balance:** Shows current White Balance setting.
23. **Film Simulation:** Shows the currently selected Film Simulation.
24. **F-Log/HLG Recording:** Shows if F-Log or HLG (Hybrid Log-Gamma) is being used.
25. **Dynamic Range:** Shows Dynamic Range setting.
26. **D-Range Priority:** Shows D-Range setting.
27. **Movie Optimized Control:** Tapping here changes the controls, dials, and touch controls for movie shooting.
28. **Boost Mode:** Improves viewfinder and AF speed. Shows if this is turned on.
29. **Temperature Warning:** Shows yellow or red as camera gets too hot. Turn camera off and wait for it to cool down.
30. **Control Lock:** Shows when controls are locked.
31. **Battery Level:** Shows power level of battery.
32. **Distance Indicator:** Shows the distance to the subject.
33. **Sensitivity (ISO):** Shows current ISO.
34. **Histogram:** Shows the histogram for the current view.
35. **Exposure Compensation:** Shows the current Exposure Compensation.
36. **Aperture:** Shows current aperture.
37. **Time Code:** Shows the current time code.
38. **Shutter Speed:** Shows current shutter speed.
39. **TTL Lock:** Shows when Flash TTL output is locked. Used to keep output consistent over a series of images (Lock with Last Flash, or Lock with Metering Flash).
40. **AE Lock:** Shows when exposure is locked.
41. **Metering:** Shows current Metering mode.
42. **Shooting Mode:** Shows current Shooting mode.
43. **Focus Mode:** Shows current Focus mode.

44. **Focus Indicator:** Shows the focus status.

( ): Camera is focusing.

• (green): Subject is in focus and locked, in S Focus mode.

(•) (green): Subject is in focus in C Focus mode, focus will adjust as subject distance changes.

(•) (blinking white): Camera is unable to find focus.

45. **Manual Focus Indicator:** Shows when you're using Manual focus.
46. **AF Lock:** Shows when autofocus is locked.
47. **Mic Jack Setting:** Shows if a microphone or line in is selected for the mic jack.
48. **AF+MF Indicator:** Shows if AF+MF is on or off.
49. **Shutter Type:** Shows which shutter type is selected.
50. **Recording Level:** Shows the current audio recording level.
51. **Continuous Mode:** Shows which Continuous mode is selected: CH (Continuous High) or CL (Continuous Low).
52. **Exposure Indicator:** In M mode it shows how different the current settings are from what the camera believes the proper exposure should be according to the current Metering mode.
53. **Self-Timer Indicator:** Shows the number of seconds remaining until the camera fires.
54. **Flash (TTL) Mode:** Shows the TTL for the EF-X8 hot shoe-mounted flash.
55. **IS (Image Stabilization) Mode:** Image Stabilization can be set to Continuous, Shooting Only (only active in Focus mode C or when the shutter is released), or Off.

03 ESSENTIAL MODES AND SETTINGS

SHOOTING MODES

P (Program AE [auto exposure]): Camera sets shutter speed and aperture for optimal exposure. Turn the Shutter Speed dial to A (auto), set the Aperture to A (auto), and confirm that P appears in the display.

S (Shutter Speed Priority): You set the shutter speed and the camera sets the aperture. Turn the Shutter Speed dial to set the shutter speed, and set the Aperture to A (auto).

T (Time): Use this mode to set slow shutter speeds for long exposures. Turn the Shutter Speed dial to T (time), then use the Rear Command dial to set the shutter speed.

B (Bulb): Use this mode to take long exposures by pressing the Shutter button all the way down to start the exposure and lifting your finger off the Shutter button to stop the exposure. Shutter can remain open for up to 60 minutes.

Note: When the Aperture is set to A (auto), the shutter speed is fixed at 30 seconds.

A (Aperture Priority): You set the aperture and the camera sets the shutter speed. Turn the Shutter Speed dial to A (auto), set the aperture to the User-Selected option (the aperture icon), then set the aperture to your desired f/stop using the aperture ring on the lens.

M (Manual): You set both the shutter speed and the aperture. Set the shutter speed using the Shutter Speed dial, and set the aperture to the User-Selected option (the aperture icon), then use the aperture ring on the lens to set the desired aperture. M will appear in the display.

METERING MODES

Shooting Settings > Photometry.

Spot: The camera meters the lighting in the center of the frame. Best for subjects where the background is really bright or really dark.

Center-Weighted: The camera looks at the whole scene but gives more emphasis to the area in the center.

Multi: The camera looks at the whole scene and tries to determine the best exposure using composition, color, and brightness. Best for most situations.

Average: The exposure is set to the average of the entire frame.

EXPOSURE COMPENSATION

Rotate the Exposure Compensation dial to adjust the exposure from –3 (darker) to +3 (lighter) stops.

Custom: Set the Exposure Compensation dial to C, then adjust the exposure compensation using the Front Command dial to adjust the exposure from –5 (darker) to +5 (lighter) stops. The Front Command dial can be used to set aperture or exposure compensation. Just press the dial to switch between the two.

FOCUS MODES

Use the Focus Mode selector to set the Focus mode.

S: AF-S (Single AF): Focus starts when Shutter button is pressed and locks when focus is achieved. Best for stationary subjects.

C: AF-C (Continuous AF): Focus starts when Shutter button is pressed halfway and continues to focus until photo is taken. Best for moving subjects.

M: Manual Focus: Focusing is accomplished by turning focusing ring on lens barrel.

[ ] AUTOFOCUS OPTIONS

Shooting Menus > AF/MF Setting > AF Mode

When in AF-S Focus mode:

Single Point: Uses single point for critical, pinpoint focus.

Zone: Camera automatically focuses on the subject in the selected focus zone. The focus zones use multiple focus points, making it easier to focus on moving subjects.

Wide: Camera focuses automatically on high-contrast subjects.

All: This allows you to use the Rear Command dial to cycle through the Single Point, Zone, and Wide AF modes when in the focus point selection display.

When in AF-C Focus mode:

Single Point: Uses single point for critical focus and tracks subject using that point. Best for subjects moving toward or away from the camera.

Zone: Camera automatically focuses on the subject in the selected focus zone. The focus zones use multiple focus points, making it easier to focus on moving subjects.

Tracking: The camera focuses automatically on the subject and tries to track it using the wide area of the frame.

All: This allows you to use the Rear Command dial to cycle through the Single Point, Zone, and Tracking AF modes when in the focus point selection display.

DRIVE SETTINGS

Turn the Drive dial to the desired setting.

Panorama: Allows you to shoot in-camera panorama images.

ADV. (Advanced filter): Navigate to Shooting Menus > Shooting Setting > Drive Setting > Adv. Filter Setting to choose from the following filters: Toy Camera, Miniature, Pop Color, High-Key, Low-Key, Dynamic Tone, Soft Focus, and multiple Partial Color options.

BKT (Bracketing): Sets the camera to shoot in bracketing mode. The Bracketing is set in the Shooting Menus > Shooting Setting > Drive Setting > BKT Setting menu. You can set the bracketing type to the following options: AE BKT (exposure bracketing), ISO BKT, Film Simulation BKT, White Balance BKT, Dynamic Range BKT, or Focus BKT.

CH (Continuous High-Speed Burst): Set the frame advance rate in the Shooting Menus > Shooting Setting > Drive Setting menu. Takes up to 30 FPS (using the electronic shutter and the 1.25 crop mode) or 11 FPS (normal shutter and full frame) for as long as you press the Shutter button.

CL (Continuous Low-Speed Burst): Takes up to 5.7 FPS for as long as you press the Shutter button.

S (Single): Takes a single frame each time the Shutter button is pressed.

HDR: Camera takes three shots of varying exposure and combines them.

WHITE BALANCE

Press the Fn5 button, which is set to White Balance by default.

White balance can be set to keep colors accurate under a variety of lighting types. The X-T4 provides the following options: Auto White Priority, Auto, Auto Ambience Priority, Custom 1-3, K (select a specific color temperature), Sunlight, Shade, Daylight Fluorescent (Fluorescent 1), Warm White Fluorescent (Fluorescent 2), Cool White Fluorescent (Fluorescent 3), Incandescent, and Underwater.

IMAGE QUALITY

Shooting Menus > I.Q. (Image Quality) Setting > Image Quality

FINE: Low compression ratio means bigger files with more detail.

NORMAL: Higher compression ratio for smaller files with less detail.

FINE + RAW: Records both a Fine JPEG and a RAW file each time the Shutter button is pressed.

NORMAL + RAW: Records both a Normal JPEG and a RAW file each time the Shutter button is pressed.

RAW: Records a RAW file only (no JPEG).

Note: RAW files can be saved as either compressed, lossless compressed, or uncompressed files.

IMAGE SIZE

Shooting Menus > I.Q. (Image Quality) Setting > Image Size

Select both the image size and the aspect ratio you want. There are three options for Aspect Ratio: 3:2, 16:9, or 1:1 square. Then you can pick a size: L (Large), M (Medium), or S (Small). The largest size and aspect ratio available is Large 3:2.

DISPLAY MODES

Press the View Mode button to cycle through the Display modes.

Eye Sensor: Putting your eye to the viewfinder turns the EVF (electronic viewfinder) on and the LCD monitor off. Removing your eye from the viewfinder turns the LCD monitor on and the EVF off.

LCD Only: LCD monitor is on and the EVF is off.

EVF Only: EVF is turned on and LCD monitor is off.

EVF Only + Eye Sensor: The EVF turns on when your eye covers the viewfinder. EVF turns off when the eye is moved away. LCD monitor remains off.

Eye Sensor + LCD Image Display: Putting your eye to the viewfinder during shooting turns the EVF on, but the LCD monitor is still used for the display of images once you remove your eye from the viewfinder after shooting.

04 OTHER HELPFUL SETTINGS

FILM SIMULATION

Shooting Menus > I.Q. (Image Quality) Setting > Film Simulation. Film Simulations re-create the look of traditional film.

Provia/Standard: Standard color for general photography.

Velvia/Vivid: High contrast and saturated colors. Ideal for nature photography.

Astia/Soft: Softer colors create a more subdued look.

Classic Chrome: Soft color and enhanced shadow contrast.

Pro Neg. Hi: Slightly increased contrast, best for portraits.

Pro Neg. Std: Soft gradations and skin tones, best for portraits.

Classic Neg: Enhanced color with harder tonality, which increases image depth.

Eterna/Cinema: Subdued soft colors and deep shadows for a film look in movies.

Eterna Bleach Bypass: Low saturation and high contrast.

Acros: Black-and-white photos with rich gradation and heightened sharpness.

Monochrome: Standard black and white.

Sepia: Sepia-toned images.

Note: The Acros and Monochrome settings also allow the addition of a yellow (Ye), red (R), or green (G) filter to adjust the contrast depending on the image's underlying colors.

COLOR SPACE

Shooting Menus > I.Q. (Image Quality) Setting > Color Space

sRGB: Smaller color space. Best when images are used directly from camera.

Adobe RGB: Larger color space. Best used for commercial printing.

NOISE REDUCTION

Shooting Menus > I.Q. (Image Quality) Setting > Noise Reduction. There are two forms of noise reduction available.

Noise Reduction: Shooting Menus > I.Q. (Image Quality) Setting > High ISO NR: Reduces noise when using high ISOs. You can choose from +4 to –4 depending on noise and taste.

Long Exposure NR: Shooting Menus > I.Q. (Image Quality) Setting > Long Exposure NR: Reduces noise and mottling in images using longer shutter speeds. Can be turned On or Off.

AUTO SENSITIVITY (ISO)

Turn sensitivity dial to A (Auto).

The sensitivity (ISO) is automatically adjusted using the settings in Shooting Menus > Shooting Setting > ISO Auto Setting. There are settings for the Default Sensitivity (160-12800), the Maximum Sensitivity (400-12800), and the Minimum Shutter Speed. You can create three combinations of settings (Auto1, Auto2, and Auto3). At their defaults, they are set to the following:

Auto1: Default Sensitivity: ISO 160, Max Sensitivity: ISO 800, Minimum Shutter Speed: AUTO.

Auto2: Default Sensitivity: ISO 160, Max Sensitivity: ISO 1600, Minimum Shutter Speed: AUTO.

Auto3: Default Sensitivity: ISO 160, Max Sensitivity: ISO 3200, Minimum Shutter Speed: AUTO.

Note: The minimum shutter speed can be set to either Auto, or between the range of 1/4 second–1/500 second.

SHOT

TOUCH SCREEN CONTROLS

The LCD monitor is touch enabled and can be used to perform a variety of functions. Enable touch controls by selecting On in Setup Menus > Button/Dial Setting > Touch Screen Setting. You can then set the following:

Touch Screen Setting: When turned on, the LCD monitor acts as a touch screen, allowing you to use it to focus and take photos by tapping once on the subject. In burst mode, the camera will continue to take photos for as long as you keep your finger on the display. When shooting movies, pressing the Shutter button stops the recording.

Double Tap Setting: Turn on to enable double tap to zoom in on the subject during playback.

Touch Function: Enables touch function gestures.

Playback Touch Screen Setting: When enabled, the LCD acts like a touch screen during playback. EVF Touch Screen Area Settings: Select the area of the LCD used for touch controls when the viewfinder is active.

ELECTRONIC LEVEL

Setup Menus > Screen Setup > Disp. Custom Setting. Highlight Electronic Level and press OK to select.

Now the display will show a virtual horizon you can use to confirm your photographs are level.

DR100 DYNAMIC RANGE

Shooting Menus > I.Q. (Image Quality) Setting > Dynamic Range

The Dynamic Range setting helps with controlling the contrast in your images. The available options are Auto, 100%, 200%, and 400%. Choose a lower value to increase contrast when shooting indoors or under a cloudy sky. Choose a higher value to reduce the loss of detail in the highlight areas when photographing high-contrast scenes.

D RANGE PRIORITY

Shooting Menus > I.Q. (Image Quality) Setting > D Range Priority. D Range Priority attempts to reduce the loss of detail in high-contrast scenes.

Auto: The contrast is adjusted automatically based on the lighting conditions.

Strong: Adjusts the dynamic range for very high-contrast scenes. Only available at ISO 640–12800.

Weak: Makes smaller adjustments to the dynamic range for moderately high-contrast scenes. Only available at ISO 320–12800.

Off: Turns the contrast reduction off.

WIRELESS COMMUNICATION

Setup Menus > Connection Setting > Bluetooth Settings > Pairing Registration

Use the FUJIFILM Camera Remote app on your smartphone or tablet to connect to the camera, allowing you to control the camera remotely, download images directly to the device, upload location information to the camera, and browse images on the device.

05 STEP-BY-STEP SHOOTING INSTRUCTIONS

PANORAMA

Create an in-camera panorama:

1. Rotate Drive dial to the Panorama icon.

2. Select the size of the angle through which you'll pan: press the selector left, highlight a size, and press MENU/OK.

3. Press the selector right to choose the pan direction. Highlight the desired pan direction and press MENU/OK.

4. Press the Shutter button all the way down to start recording your pano. (You don't need to hold down the Shutter button for the duration of the shot.)

5. Pan the camera in the direction shown by the arrow.

6. Shooting ends when the camera has panned to the end of the guides.

For best results, use a focal length of 50mm or less and move the camera at a steady, slow speed.

MULTIPLE EXPOSURE

Create an in-camera multiple exposure from multiple photos:

1. Shooting Setting > Multiple Exposure to ON and pick from the following blend modes:

   Additive: Camera adds exposures together.

   Average: Camera automatically optimizes exposure for the final image.

   Bright: Camera looks at all the exposures and picks the brightest pixel for each.

   Dark: Camera looks at all exposures and picks the darkest pixel for each.

2. Take the first photo.
3. Press MENU/OK and the first shot will be shown superimposed on the view through the lens. (If you want to retake the first shot, press the selector to the left.)
4. Take the second shot.
5. Press MENU/OK to combine the exposures. (If you want to retake this photo, press the selector to the left.)
6. Make additional exposures, up to nine images total.
7. When done, press the DISP/BACK button to end shooting and create the final multiple exposure.

Note: Multiple exposures cannot be created when shooting tethered.

INTERVAL TIMER PHOTOGRAPHY

Set your X-T4 to take a series of photos over a period of time:

1. Select Shooting Menus > Shooting Setting > Interval Timer Shooting.
2. Use the selector to choose the interval and the number of shots. Press MENU/OK.
3. Use the selector to choose the starting time, then press MENU/OK. The shooting will begin automatically.

06 TYPICAL SHOOTING SCENARIOS

SHOOTING SCENARIO
PORTRAIT

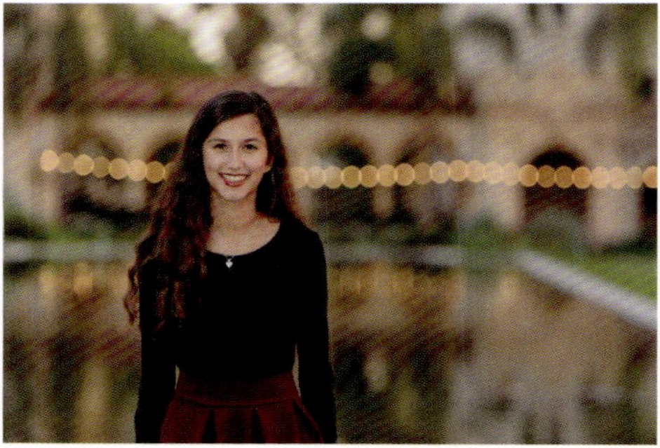

KEY PRINCIPLES

- The key to a portrait like this is shallow depth of field. So shoot in **APERTURE PRIORITY** mode. Turn the Shutter Speed dial to A (auto), then set the aperture to the User-Selected option (the aperture icon), and use the lens aperture ring to adjust the aperture. Start with the lowest aperture your lens offers (such as **f/2.8 or f/4**).
- Remember to **focus on the eyes**.

- If the image is too dark or too light, use **EXPOSURE COMPENSATION** to adjust the brightness level.
- If the image is blurry from a slow shutter speed, **raise the ISO** to increase your sensor's sensitivity to light, thus allowing for a faster shutter speed.
- Remember to use a **focal length of 50mm or greater** so that you don't distort your subject's face.

SHOOTING SCENARIO
GROUP PORTRAIT

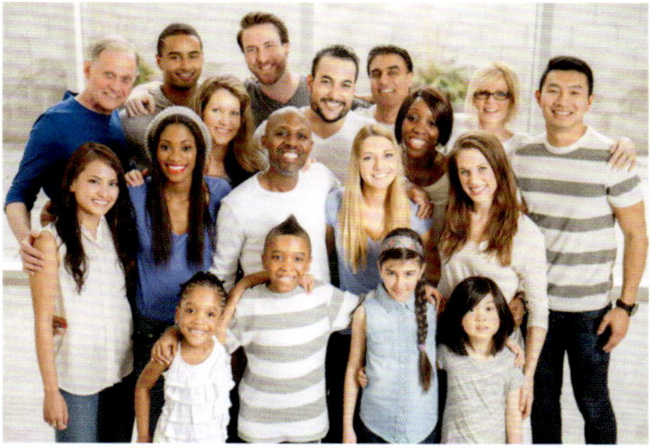

KEY PRINCIPLES

- In order to get everyone in focus, you need a deep depth of field. So shoot in **APERTURE PRIORITY** mode. Turn the Shutter Speed dial to A (auto), then set the aperture to the User-Selected option (the aperture icon), and use the lens aperture ring to adjust the aperture. Set the aperture between **f/8–f/16**.
- **Focus on the person in the middle of the group**. Check focus by zooming in to view it at 100% and check the faces in the group. If anyone is out of focus, use a smaller aperture for deeper depth of field.
- Use **MULTI METERING** mode to account for the light in the entire scene.
- **Arrange the group so they can all see you** (and you can see them).
- Use **EXPOSURE COMPENSATION** if the image is too bright or too dark.
- If the image is blurry, **raise the ISO** to allow the camera to use a faster shutter speed.

LANDSCAPE

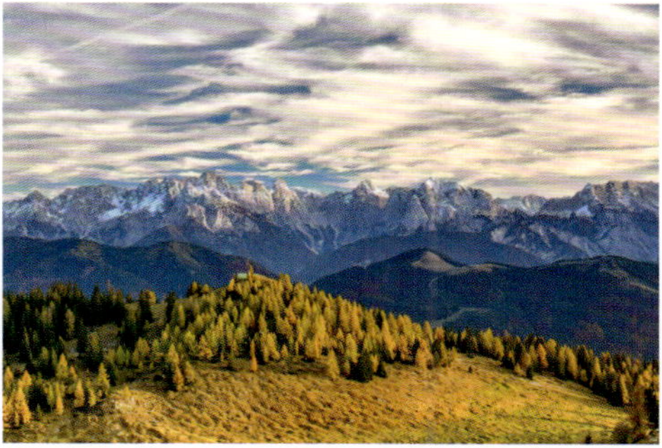

KEY PRINCIPLES

- Shoot in **APERTURE PRIORITY** to control depth of field. Turn the Shutter Speed dial to A (auto), then set the aperture to the User-Selected option (the aperture icon), and use the lens aperture ring to adjust the aperture. Start with **f/16** to ensure deep depth of field.

- **Use a tripod** to eliminate camera movement. Whenever your camera is on a tripod, also make sure **IMAGE STABILIZATION** is turned off.
- Use **MULTI METERING** mode and **SINGLE AUTOFOCUS (AF-S)**.
- **Set the ISO to a low setting (160–200)** to avoid any digital noise.
- Shoot in **RAW** so that you have the most available information when editing later.
- Consider **BRACKETING** your exposures.

SHOOTING SCENARIO

FREEZE ACTION

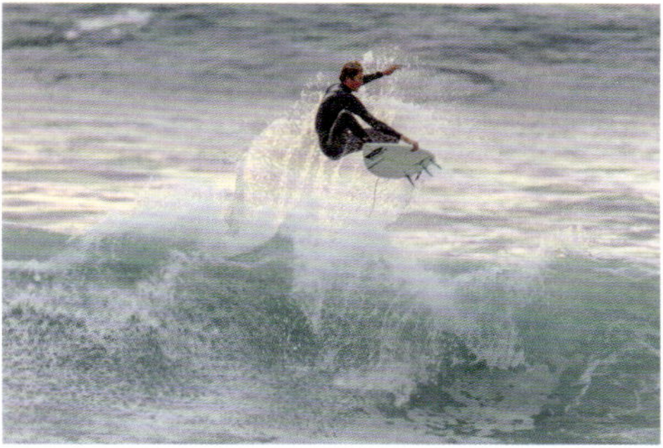

KEY PRINCIPLES

- Use **SHUTTER PRIORITY** mode. Set the aperture to Auto and set the shutter speed to a value that will freeze the action. The appropriate shutter speed depends on your subject and its movement, but could be anywhere between **1/500–1/8000 sec**.
- Use **CONTINUOUS AUTOFOCUS (AF-C)** so that the camera keeps focusing as the subject moves.
- If the image is dark or blurry, **raise the ISO** or try AUTO ISO to automatically have the camera adjust the ISO as needed.

SHOOTING SCENARIO

SHOWING MOTION—PANNING

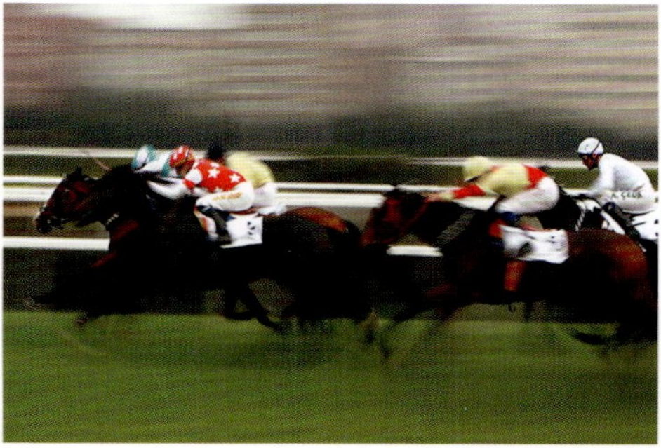

KEY PRINCIPLES

- Shoot in **SHUTTER PRIORITY** mode. Set the aperture to Auto and set the shutter speed to a value that is slow enough to allow for the subject to move during the exposure.
- **Follow the subject** across the frame as you shoot.
- Try **LIVE VIEW**, which allows you to see the subject during the exposure.
- Use **CONTINUOUS AUTOFOCUS (AF-C)**, as well as **TRACKING AF**.

SHOOTING SCENARIO

LOW-LIGHT ACTION

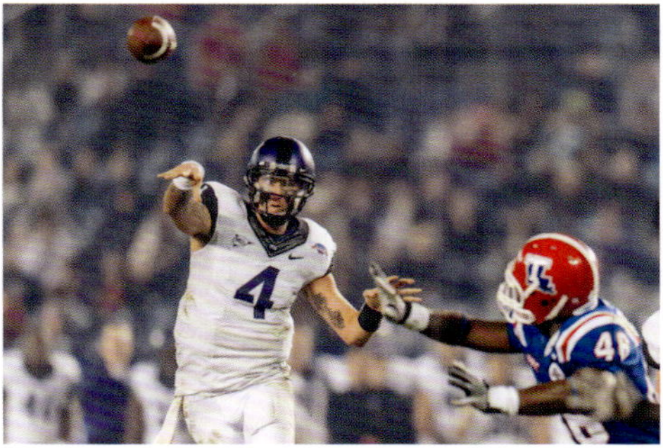

KEY PRINCIPLES

- Shoot in **APERTURE PRIORITY** mode and use a wide aperture such as **f/2.8 or f/4**. Turn the Shutter Speed dial to A (auto), then set the aperture to the User-Selected option (the aperture icon), and use the lens aperture ring to adjust the aperture.
- Use **SPOT METERING** and meter on the subject's face.
- Use **CONTINUOUS AUTOFOCUS (AF-C)** and **SINGLE POINT AF**.
- **Set the ISO to 1600 or higher**, depending on the amount of available light.
- If the image is blurry, **increase the ISO** to allow for a faster shutter speed.

SHOOTING SCENARIO

LONG EXPOSURE

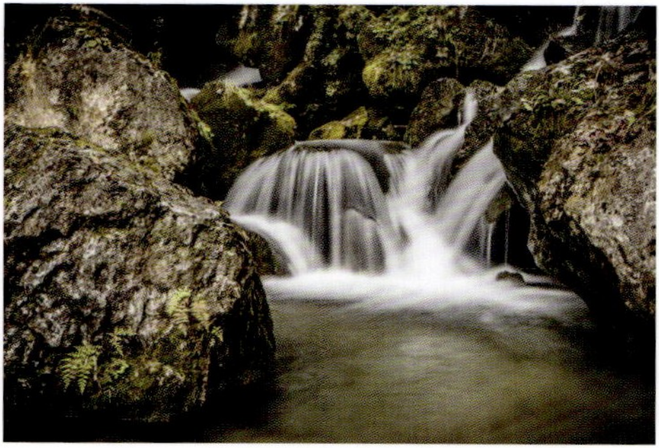

KEY PRINCIPLES

- Rotate the **Shutter Speed dial to T or B** and the aperture to anything other than A (Auto). This allows you to use a long shutter speed.
- **Use a tripod** and a **remote release** to keep the camera stable. **Turn off IMAGE STABILIZATION**.
- Use the **SINGLE AUTOFOCUS (AF-S)** Focus mode, or try manual focus if the camera is having a hard time locking on focus.
- **Use a low ISO** (160–400) and **shoot RAW**.